S0-BYQ-861

Hi Lowell,

Enjoy our latest book "Journey of Love"!

Wishing You Love, Peace, Happiness, Joy & Peace.

Marty Cole & Aurora Belderol

P.S. Please tell your friends about our book. Thank-You!

Praise for Marty and Aurora and *Journey of Love*

I'm honored to recommend *Journey of Love*. It was written by two extraordinary people who have taught me the meaning of friendship and love. Aurora writes as lyrically as she performs as a musician. Aurora shares her amazing journey from the Philippines to becoming an American business owner and matriarch of a beautiful and talented family. The love she shares with my dear friend Marty has helped healed his life. They are both deeply spiritual beings lighting up our world.

—Patti Higgins, friend

Journey of Love is sure to inspire each reader to accept the guidance of one's own divine spirit and embrace a life of peace with purpose. We all need to be reminded to use and apply life's tool kit of positivity. Marty and Aurora's life journeys separate and together are clear examples of gratitude and kindness. A book that offers a simple but powerful message, live a life of peace.

—Ellie Vargas Page, Wisdom Healing student of six years

I have known Aurora since kindergarten. We grew up together sharing friends and school until we parted ways to pursue our passions and respond to our respective callings. Her stories are repositories of historical memories, topped with gems of values and realizations learned along the way.

Both Aurora and Marty have become tale bearers of their own truths, and have distilled their experiences to become useful to those who hope to continue their own journey in joy, love and peace.

—Myrna T. Pagsuberon, Lawyer, Philippines

Reading this narrative *Journey of Love,* one cannot help be fascinated of Aurora and Marty who traveled on their own divergent paths, then wound up at a crossroad where fate aligned their stars.

The best that I can articulate of my friendship with Aurora is none other than my encounters with her. Encounter in a sense that goes beyond knowing someone, and having the privilege of entering into the heart of a person. I have the honor of being with her in both happy and challenging moments of her life. I have seen her go through it all with calmness, gentleness, and inner confidence of herself.

Steve Jobs once said, "Your time is limited, don't waste it living someone else's life." Aurora is authentic. Hear her play the piano, watch her dance, enjoy her laughter with friends, and see her face beaming with pride for her family! That's Aurora!

Usually when you are in the company of lovers, three is a crowd, one feels out of place. Not so when I am with Aurora and Marty. With Marty's gift of discourse, we skillfully drift from one topic to another. I have enjoyed their company many times. I see each of them bring out the best of each other – a good match!

So Aurora and Marty, keep each of your otherness and enjoy your togetherness.

I pray for you with St. Paul's words: "May the grace of the Lord Jesus Christ, the Love of God and the fellowship of the Holy Spirit be with both of you."

Fe Musgrave, friend

Memoirs and Life Lessons

Journey
of Love

MARTY COLE AND
AURORA BELDEROL

BALBOA.PRESS
A DIVISION OF HAY HOUSE

Copyright © 2020 Marty Cole and Aurora Belderol.

All rights reserved. No part of this book may be used or reproduced by any means, graphic, electronic, or mechanical, including photocopying, recording, taping or by any information storage retrieval system without the written permission of the author except in the case of brief quotations embodied in critical articles and reviews.

Balboa Press books may be ordered through booksellers or by contacting:

Balboa Press
A Division of Hay House
1663 Liberty Drive
Bloomington, IN 47403
www.balboapress.com
844-682-1282

Because of the dynamic nature of the Internet, any web addresses or links contained in this book may have changed since publication and may no longer be valid. The views expressed in this work are solely those of the author and do not necessarily reflect the views of the publisher, and the publisher hereby disclaims any responsibility for them.

The author of this book does not dispense medical advice or prescribe the use of any technique as a form of treatment for physical, emotional, or medical problems without the advice of a physician, either directly or indirectly. The intent of the author is only to offer information of a general nature to help you in your quest for emotional and spiritual well-being. In the event you use any of the information in this book for yourself, which is your constitutional right, the author and the publisher assume no responsibility for your actions.

Any people depicted in stock imagery provided by Getty Images are models, and such images are being used for illustrative purposes only.
Certain stock imagery © Getty Images.

Cover photograph is property of Preservation Partners of the Fox Valley.
Photo titled "Moon Bridge at the Fabyan Japanese Garden".

Print information available on the last page.

ISBN: 978-1-9822-5272-4 (sc)
ISBN: 978-1-9822-5274-8 (hc)
ISBN: 978-1-9822-5273-1 (e)

Library of Congress Control Number: 2020914765

Balboa Press rev. date: 10/02/2020

Acknowledgments

Our Special Thanks to:
Mary Oxley and her team at Balboa Press
Daniel Cobo, our assistant
And to our families for all their love and support

Cover photograph is property of Preservation
Partners of the Fox Valley
Photo title: "Moon Bridge at the Fabyan Japanese Garden"

Symbolic Meaning of Front Cover
Two swans forming a heart: love
Bridge: journey, communication and connectedness
Trees: transformation, strength and growth
Green color: unconditional love, abundance, harmony and healing

This book is dedicated
to our loved ones
and all kindred souls.

Contents

Foreword

What do an accomplished pianist from a small island in the Philippines and a dynamic sales professional from Southern California have in common? Well, you'd be surprised. On paper, they may seem as far apart as the vast ocean that spans their places of birth. In reality, they harmoniously serve as one another's most intimate reflection of all that life has inspired them to become.

My name is Lorenzo. I am the proud son of Aurora, and it is my distinct honor to be the tone-setter of this timeless meditation. It is the journey of two kindred spirits from opposite sides of the world, destined by grace and united by joy, music, and the soul's unrelenting urge toward spiritual fulfillment.

As our society influences us to become more polarized and isolated from each other, *Journey of Love* gives us insight into the perspective of another to reveal that we are inherently more alike than we are different. We all want to love and be genuinely loved in return. We each want to feel that our lives have purpose. And for many of us, we are called by the whispering voice in our hearts that invites us toward our spiritual awakening.

Although *Journey of Love* is the memoir and life lessons of two unique individuals, in actuality it's one story—the story that each of us, as divine spiritual beings having human experience, are all currently living. It is our narrative as consciousness, told through the individual lenses of Aurora and Marty celebrating what it means to be alive.

There are no words to describe my immense admiration for my mother and Marty for completing this book. My mom, who is usually a very private person, had to break through and transcend the fears that many of us undoubtedly face when conveying our innermost thoughts and feelings. Having been a firsthand witness to my mom's personal evolution, I see this book as a testament to the high self-worth instilled by her parents. It is this belief in herself that gave her the strength to overcome insurmountable obstacles and become a successful and independent businesswoman. With her invaluable gifts of music and performance, she inspires all those around her with the confidence to sing their own authentic melodies.

As the great 13th century Sufi poet Rumi wrote, "The wound is the place where the Light enters you." Marty has transformed the numerous challenges placed upon him and walks courageously, embodying a beacon of light and empowerment that is visible to all he encounters. His poignant message of letting go of fear and embracing the love all around us could not be more relevant today. Marty's immense positive influence and unwavering belief in improving the life of others is beautifully exemplified by his two previous inspirational books, *My Amazing Transformation of Love, Courage, and Wisdom* and *My Love Story Book of Poetry*. I highly recommend you check those out as well!

I have learned so much and continue to grow with every meaningful encounter with these two blessed beings. Now I graciously invite you to come along on this bliss-filled journey, a *Journey of Love*.

—Lorenzo Caunan

PART I

AURORA'S STORY

Introduction

The Epiphany

It was New Year's Day 2018. In a vortex of joy from a spectacular celebration with my family, I had the inspiration to write my story and share the hard-won years of spiritual growth life has taught me. In a few months, I was going to turn seventy. Still with childlike wonder, I was excited about a new milestone happening soon, for I have always felt age is just a state of mind.

It's my belief that with age comes wisdom and inner beauty. When you embrace the wisdom life gives you and treat every bump in the road with courage and dignity, you feel empowered and ageless. To feel ageless is to be in a constant game of learning and traveling through life with ease and grace.

Because we are the authors of our own life stories, it's up to us how we want our stories to shine. Everything is about the choices we make, and how we deal with life's challenges makes the difference. We are the creators and the alchemists as we make our transformations to our own awakenings.

My contribution is in the area of interpreting what I have learned from spiritual masters and applying them to my own experiences. I embrace a calm, positive attitude. Life has not exempted me from turbulent times, but it has taught me to go with the flow and look for the wisdom behind it. The movie of my life is based on how I embrace my own truth and, from this vantage point, learn to dance to life's syncopated rhythms in my own peaceful way.

Sharing our life stories is cathartic and fulfilling. It is a growing experience that gives us a panoramic view of where we have been, where we are right now, and where we are going. It also gives us a better perspective on the people in our lives and why they are there. Sharing our stories makes us find our true selves. It is a priceless legacy to leave to our loved ones and future generations—the lessons embedded in our souls.

According to spiritual teachers, the soul or the consciousness within each of us is where the true self resides. It is the essence of who we really are, free from the layers of masks that we put upon ourselves in different situations and for different people. The soul is the higher self, the god within us. When we listen to the voice in our souls, we're moved to be inspired, creative, and loving to our fellow earth travelers. Our souls are infinite and will stay forever when our physical bodies die.

I am thankful to my soul partner Marty for planting the seed that I share my story. He is a beautiful soul, full of passion to make a difference in people's lives by spreading his message of love and compassion for others. He and I collaborated in writing *Journey of Love* to share the different paths we have followed that led us to a life of unconditional love. Although we have opposite personalities with different lifestyles, our spiritual journey has brought balance and alignment to our lives, bringing love, peace, and harmony to ourselves and to others.

To us all, ages seventeen to seventy-one and beyond: may we make our unique paths a contribution to the world.

Chapter 1

A DIVINE PURPOSE

I magine you are at a concert, listening to a Beethoven concerto. A piano soloist is performing with an orchestra, and a conductor is leading the whole performance. Altogether, you hear a perfect blending of beautiful music, and you feel uplifted in your soul. As an accomplished pianist, that's how I look at life—like a concerto.

In life, you are the soloist, the creator of the melody that makes you unique. You play the music in your soul that only you can play. You don't let anyone define who you truly are. With confidence, you walk your own path and follow your dreams. As you use your God-given free will to choose what's best for you, you tap into your inner wisdom for guidance. You use this power to be the best that you can be and be the master of your own destiny.

The performers in the orchestra of your life are your family, friends, and mentors supporting you in your journey. I was blessed to be raised in a God-centered family and to attend a school that taught me the teachings of Jesus, which has enhanced the values I learned from home. My upbringing gave me a strong foundation that has been useful to me. These days, my life is deeply inspired by the wisdom of Abraham-Esther Hicks, Wayne Dyer, Deepak Chopra, Louise Hay, Sonia Choquette, Eckhart Tolle, Jon Kabat-Zinn, and Don Miguel Ruiz. These masters have taught me practical ways to live in today's society through awareness, meditation, love, and compassion for others.

God, our Divine Source, is the Divine Conductor of our lives. When we follow His lead, life becomes a masterpiece of art. Life is about living our truth and having love—love for ourselves, for others, and above all for our Divine Source. We are all beautiful extensions of divine energy, and this energy is the source of our power. When we embrace the divine in us, life becomes heaven on earth. We find love, peace, and joy within.

No matter how smart we are, if we are not connected to our Divine Source, we can't fully express who we truly are. Life gives us the ability to manifest what we want as we accept the flow of the Spirit of the Divine Source within us. Here is a simple example: whenever I perform at concerts, I let this divine energy channel through me. In doing so, I feel the divine expressing itself through my music as my fingers gently glide over the piano keys.

Loving yourself is about honoring your true self and your values. You are at peace with yourself and content being who you are. You know who you are and what you want. You do what you are here for.

Living your true self allows you to travel through life as the divine being you are meant to be. You are calm as you face life's highs and lows. You are able to love others unconditionally, without any hidden agenda. You surround yourself with people who inspire you to your highest potential. You don't give anyone permission to rob you of the joy of living when they are mean or judgmental of you. People's insecurities are none of your business.

As spiritual beings presently in this physical life, we are in this journey together, connected through the amazing power of God's love. We are all searching for our true path, and each of us serves as an instrument to fulfill our divine purpose. As we cross paths with our fellow earth travelers, they are there for one reason: to make us grow in love and wisdom as we serve one another.

I am very grateful for my blessings. In my concerto of life, I have achieved what I wanted to do. I have a family of three successful children who have blessed me with five adorable grandchildren. Through the years, I have peacefully navigated my journey by honoring what I am here to be: a vessel of love and service to others through the use of my talents and gifts.

Chapter 2

TREASURES FROM CHILDHOOD

The lessons children bring into our lives are priceless. They are having fun living in the moment and do not worry about the past or the future. When we look through their innocent eyes, they teach us pure love and joy.

I believe we are the sum total of every experience we have had, and our childhood experiences help shape who we are today. As children, we get a lot of love and attention from our parents. Unfortunately, some of us did not feel loved and sometimes end up struggling to find love for the rest of our lives. Yet we do not need to blame our parents or a challenging childhood for our own issues. We all experience hurts and disappointments. By being in the driver's seat and taking responsibility for ourselves, we can shine our best in life, for each of us is the genie we are looking for in our own world.

I come from a culture in which the love of God and strong family values are deeply ingrained in our hearts. Parents and elders are treated with deep respect. Children look up to them for guidance and take care of them in their old age. We have a beautiful tradition we call *mano po* that we practice to honor them. It is a form of greeting. We take an elder's right hand, and with our heads bowed, we press the hand to our forehead as a way of requesting a blessing.

The Filipino people are hospitable, courteous, and caring toward one another. Good-natured and fun-loving, we celebrate life and express ourselves best through music. In many families, it's not unusual to find a budding guitarist, pianist, or singer. Music is the language of our souls. I was born and raised in the Philippines, and I was blessed to grow up in this environment.

The Philippines is an archipelago that comprises 7,641 islands. Our culture is a blend of Filipino and Spanish traditions, with strong American and Chinese influences. We have many Spanish words in our dialects, since we were ruled by Spain for 333 years, from 1565 to 1898. Up to the 1950s, a familiar mode of transportation in the towns was the *calesa*, a horse-drawn two-wheeled carriage. I remember riding in them up to the time I was about nine years old. The calesa was introduced to us in the eighteenth century by the Spaniards. Now it is mainly used as a tourist attraction.

The Philippines is predominantly Catholic. It is a third-world country where more than a quarter of the population lives in poverty. Good jobs are hard to find if one does not have a college education. It is common for upper middle class families to hire housemaids and even drivers, since unemployment is prevalent among the uneducated.

Bohol, the province where I come from, has grown dramatically from what it used to be. Through the years, tourism has been developed and has economically improved the lives of our people. Nature has gifted us with white sandy beaches on the small island of Panglao, and the "chocolate hills" majestically nestle the town of Carmen. During summertime, these naturally cone-shaped hills turn brown like huge chocolate drops, a world wonder for tourists to explore. They were my favorite sight as a young child, whenever our family passed the hills on our way to visit our farm close by.

Many years ago, in my peaceful hometown of Tagbilaran, the capital of Bohol, everybody knew everyone. Families were close-knit. The people were God-centered and cared for one another. Pedro, my father, was a role model, not only to me but also to our townspeople, whom he served as mayor for many years. He served selflessly, and his compassion for the poor endeared him to our townspeople. Coming from humble beginnings, he rose to become a successful lawyer whose name remained untarnished for his whole career.

Felicitas, my mother, was a kindhearted soul who served as a nurse in our community. While my father was gregarious, with a great sense of humor, my mother had a quiet confidence that people sometimes misconstrued as coldness. Yet my parents' opposite personalities blended beautifully into a harmonious relationship that made them one soul for the rest of their lives.

Mama's strong character was admirable and intimidating at the same time. A woman of few words, she imposed discipline with a stern look whenever she disapproved of my behavior. She was a neat freak and kept our house tidy. Our houseboy polished the floor, using a coconut husk, every single day. Each night before bedtime, Mama led the family in prayer as we knelt before an image of Jesus and Mary.

I had two older brothers, Arthur and Peter, who cared for me deeply, and a younger sister, Lucy, who died when she was only three years old. Arthur was smart and followed all the rules at home, while my adorable middle brother Peter loved to do exactly the opposite. Playful and adventurous as a child, he sometimes got spankings from my mom for breaking house rules, which made me really sad.

Arthur and Peter bonded closely and were always there for each other. In college, Arthur started medical school but had to quit when my father suddenly died. He ended up finishing a business degree and took responsibility for our family.

On the other hand, Peter continued to be rebellious in his teens, causing a lot of problems for us. But he easily got away with his mischief, charming everyone with his humorous, sunny disposition. Remarkably, in his later years, he took care of our mother until she died. On his sixty-ninth birthday, he celebrated what would be his last days on earth at an orphanage, cheering along with the orphans as they sang "Happy Birthday" to him. Each orphan was wearing a shirt with the words "Happy Birthday, Peter," which he had donated to them. That was my brother's way of saying goodbye to everyone. Friends remember him for his generosity and colorful life.

One early dawn, my expectant mother was awakened from a dream. In the dream, she saw vivid greenish light in the sky. Wondering what that was about, she woke my father. I think that got them excited. Moments later, my father rushed Mama to the hospital, and I was born. My parents later learned that the unusual light my mom saw in her dream was the aurora borealis, a light that appears in the northern sky.

Weeks later, when I was baptized, the priest told my parents that the Catholic church had canonized a new Italian saint by the name of Gemma Galgani, and he suggested that I be named in her honor. That's how I got my name: Gemma Aurora.

My sister Lucy was born four years later. I dearly enjoyed her as my playmate for a few years. Sadly, she died of "H Fever," an epidemic in our country at that time, spread by mosquitoes and other insects. That was a very tragic time for our family, and losing a sister was difficult for my young mind to comprehend.

My mother was so devastated at the loss of my sister, she became overprotective of me. As a child, I felt like I was Rapunzel from a fairy tale book. Rapunzel's mother kept her in a tower. That's how I felt Mama showed her love for me. She kept me away from playmates for fear of me getting sick. I was spoiled by having maids take care of my needs as well as having a driver take me to school every day.

Mama threw a big birthday party for me every year, which my friends always looked forward to. During one of my class reunions, a former classmate told me that she used to enjoy watching me come to school, alighting from our family car in my neat blue-and-white school uniform, shiny shoes, and white ribbon in my hair.

Growing up in a small community had a strong bonding effect on us as kids. I had mostly the same classmates from kindergarten through high school, which caused us to treat each other like family. Through technology, we have been able to find each other again over the past decade, and we have fantastic times at our reunions, reminiscing about our childhood years.

At a recent reunion, a former classmate recollected that when we were about eight years old, she and a few of our classmates visited me at home while my parents were at work. We decided to go swimming in the fishpond in our backyard, filled with the tilapias and water lilies. We were unmindful of the murky, muddy water. Who cared? We frolicked with laughter, trying to catch the tilapias with our bare hands. What was the most fun was that my parents never knew what we did. Even my grandma who lived with us kept our mischief a secret. She just gave me a long, hot bath and told me never to do it again.

At another time, I had a get-together with a few of my schoolmates who live here in the US. One classmate told an anecdote about my mother forbidding me to go to "K of C." Marty, who was with us, was shocked and asked, "What? Your mother forbade you to eat Kentucky Fried Chicken?" Everyone burst with laughter. Little did he know that Kentucky Fried Chicken did not exist in our little town. "K of C" was a bowling center owned by the Knights of Columbus, a Catholic men's group that did charitable service in the community.

The reunion with my childhood friends was nostalgic. I felt like I was a child again in my hometown many years ago. We promised each other we'd keep in touch.

Despite all the privileges given to me growing up, my mother kept me grounded by reminding me to be humble at all times and not prove anything to anybody. Being a child, I took my parents' love and care as a norm of life. I thought everyone was good, kind, and caring. I realize now that these values are in short supply in the real world, and I'm very grateful that my parents treated everyone with love and respect. They modeled for me the values that are now ingrained in my soul and have become my source of strength at challenging times.

Looking back, I also realize I missed out on a playful childhood—but that did not matter, for I found my own playmate through the piano. Once I started taking piano lessons at seven years old, our house vibrated with music. I spent hours fine-tuning my most cherished friend. I enjoyed practicing every day and accompanying my mother when she sang her favorite songs. Although she did not have any proper vocal training, her sweet, angelic voice was inspiring to me and made me feel closer to her.

Those cherished memories still echo in my soul today. I know that was the best way Mama showed her love for me. She was not affectionate, but the music that she planted in my soul nurtured me and allowed me to grow a musical garden in my life.

When people discovered my musical versatility when I was only eight years old, they started featuring me at concerts, as well as at receptions to entertain dignitaries who were visiting our hometown. At that young age, I knew in my heart that I was born to give music to the world.

Chapter 3

HONORING MY FATHER'S LEGACY

I think of my father, Pedro, and I am transported back to my carefree childhood days. Whenever I was not practicing the piano, my favorite pastime was catching a rainbow of dragonflies that hovered around our fishpond. Some lucky days, I would have special moments with my father when he joined me. An amazing storyteller, he mesmerized me with his stories. I was most fascinated by his stories about growing up.

My father's stories about his impoverished childhood touched me deeply. He told me he never got to wear shoes until he was twelve years old. He hiked a kilometer to school each day, barefoot on a dirt road. Sometimes his feet would bleed when he stepped on sharp rocks. This did not discourage him from going to school. Instead, it motivated him to study hard and excel.

Fortunately, my father's efforts were rewarded when he graduated as valedictorian from elementary school, which ended at eighth grade. During his valedictory address, Manuel, one of the parents in the audience, was impressed by the boy's speech. He became curious when he noticed my father's strong resemblance to him. After the ceremonies, he congratulated my father and asked him where his mother was. My father told him that Josefa, his mother, had to work that day. Upon hearing the mother's name,

Manuel was moved to tears and was convinced that my father was his long-lost son.

Manuel and Josefa had had a brief relationship when Josefa worked as a housemaid for Manuel and his family after Manuel's first wife died. When Josefa discovered that she was going to have a baby, she suddenly disappeared and hid herself from everybody. Sadly, women in those days who got pregnant out of wedlock were considered disgraced and were ostracized from society.

A touching reunion took place between my father and my grandfather's family. They happily took Pedro in to live with them, and he became one of the eleven kids in the family. Another happy ending to this story was that my father got his first pair of shoes and no longer had to walk barefoot to school. He also got a lot of loving from my grandpa's second wife, Carmen, who treated him like her own son. Josefa by then had gotten married to someone else and had another son to take care of.

Papa, as I fondly called my father, was my number-one fan. Not only did he support me in my love for music, he also taught me poems that I would recite during the children's hour on our local radio station. Being an amazing poet and orator himself, he also trained me to be an orator for a contest on a national hero's day. I became the youngest champion ever in our hometown. When I graduated as an honor student from elementary school, Papa, who was the commencement speaker, beamed with pride for my accomplishment.

My father served our town as mayor for twelve years. During his tenure in office, he was voted one of the best mayors in our province for having accomplished a lot of projects, like improving infrastructure. He and our president at that time were friends. They both came from the same province, and the president, who had a residence near our house, sometimes attended our get-togethers. He and my father came from opposing political parties, and the president tried to persuade my father to change to his party. But my father, being a faithful person, humbly told the president that he would remain loyal to the party he led. The next election year, the president personally campaigned against my father, and that sadly caused my father to lose the election.

I was a college freshman studying for a degree in music when my father suddenly died of a heart attack. The evening before he died, I had a weird premonition that something bad was going to happen to him. In our backyard, our dog Brownie howled like he had seen a ghost. When I told my father about my fears, he calmly reassured me; if he were to die that night, he would let me know what the afterlife was like. At three o'clock that morning, I was awakened by the sound of my father desperately gasping for breath. We all went to his side and cried as we saw his eyes wander. When the doctor arrived, he was already gone.

On the day of his funeral, the whole town grieved over the loss of a beloved leader, as I could see from the long procession of mourners on the streets. I was moved by the astounding testimonials from our townspeople about how my father was a strong defender of the poor and the oppressed. They talked about how he rendered his legal services for free, and they in turn showed gratitude by giving our family produce that they raised in their backyards. People also described how my father was a peacemaker. He counseled couples that were having domestic problems.

I felt a lot of sadness about losing someone I loved so dearly. But that same night, I saw my father in a dream. He was standing tall in a white suit. He told me not to be sad, for he was in a happy place. He waved his hand and disappeared. Weeping tears of joy, I awoke feeling totally at peace. Always true to his word, Papa had visited me to fulfill his promise.

About three years later, for my graduation piano recital at the College of the Holy Spirit in Manila, Philippines, my mother rewarded me for my achievement by hiring a philharmonic orchestra to accompany me in my piano concerto. There were three hundred guests that night. Mama and my two brothers were in the front row, so proud of me. Beside Mama was an empty seat to honor my father's spirit. I felt Papa in my soul. It was my best performance ever. The celebration continued with a dinner reception and dance at a classy restaurant. It was a night to remember—except that I was missing Papa.

When I got back to the dormitory at midnight, some of the boarders told me that a gentleman wearing a white suit mysteriously appeared in the hallway, calling for me, while I was out celebrating with our guests. Their description resembled the image of my father. Cold chills ran down my spine; I was feeling my father's spirit. I was convinced that Papa wanted me to know that he was with me.

My father left an imprint in my soul to live my truth every day. He taught me that success is not to be measured in terms of how much money a person makes, but rather in terms of a person's integrity and how they treat people.

About ten years ago, visiting Tagbilaran, my hometown, I went to the new city hall, where my father's portrait hung on a wall. I proceeded to Belderol Street, which was named in his honor. I still feel his spirit looking after me to this day. Pedro Belderol, my father and hero, was well-loved because he served our people with integrity and compassion for the poor. He left us a legacy that, no matter where we come from, we have the power to rise above anything and be victors in life, not victims.

Chapter 4

LIFE'S HARMONIES AND DISCORDS

Going down memory lane to my youth in the late 1960s, I have fond recollections of men in our culture treating ladies with courtesy and deep respect. The maidens were modest and proper, as is shown in our cultural dances. One beautiful courtship tradition we used to have was the *harana*. A lover would woo his beloved by serenading her on moonlit nights with endearing love songs, accompanied by strums on his guitar.

Those times were unforgettable, and I appreciated the gentleman who professed his love for me through songs. Sadly, this custom has faded away. My once-quiet hometown is now bustling with people, cars, pedicabs, and motorcycles, even at night. And the gentleman in my young life turned out to be a poignant story of love lost, as fate meant it to be.

I was twenty-three years old when I first met Carlos (not his real name). Although we came from the same hometown, I hadn't met him growing up, since he was several years older than me. But I heard good things about him from my brothers. They were schoolmates. Our fathers were good friends, and both were prominent lawyers in our town.

I was enamored of Carlos's dashing personality and air of confidence. He was a successful lawyer too. After we had dated for six months, he came to my family to ask for my hand for marriage.

They all loved him, and they gave us their blessings to marry. We had a quiet, simple Catholic wedding a few months later, and we settled in Manila, the capital of the Philippines, where he was a partner in a law firm.

Carlos was a good husband. He was loving, thoughtful, and caring to the family. He treated me well, and we were happy raising our three children, Mia, Lulu, and Lorenzo. On weekends, we bonded with our relatives, as our kids enjoyed playing with their cousins. We had the conveniences of housemaids and a driver at our beck and call. They all lived with us, in separate quarters on our property.

Yet when our kids were of school age, Carlos and I decided to immigrate to the United States. This was due to the political tensions happening in our home country, which made us feel concerned about the future. There were many demonstrations, as people showed their discontent for the leaders who were in power at that time.

My parents had looked up to the US, because Americans saved our country from devastation in World War II. I had heard many horrible stories about the Japanese torturing and killing Filipinos, as well as burning their homes. When General Douglas MacArthur came to the Philippines to save us, he became our hero. My mother, who had just given birth to my eldest brother, named him Arthur in the general's honor. Those memories motivated me to convince Carlos to migrate to the US, to have a peaceful and brighter future for our family.

It was painful leaving behind my relatives, friends, and country. Tears were shed as I saw my mother waving from afar when our airplane took off. Little did I know that that would be the last time I saw Mama. She died a few years later of liver cancer.

I felt a premonition the day my mom passed away. I was home alone. A toy bird was eerily chirping in my son's room. My car, which was parked in the garage, honked by itself. I was very much alarmed to find no one was there, yet all the lights were flashing. Then I got a call from my brother Arthur telling me the sad news. He said mournfully that Mama had been calling for me before her last breath. Deeply grief-stricken, I consoled myself that Mama had visited me in spirit to say goodbye through the signs I experienced that day.

Carlos practiced law while I taught music. Like most Filipino families, we were closely bonded and loved music. Our favorite family time was having the kids gather around the grand piano, singing their hearts out, while I enjoyed accompanying them. Carlos too loved to sing and would entertain us with his own rendition of Frank Sinatra favorites. Eventually, we did family concerts, which were a lot of fun.

Raising the children in a new culture, Carlos and I managed to instill in them the values and traditions of home. Having come from a sheltered childhood, I learned to allow them the freedom to grow and explore life creatively, trusting them with the choices they made. As a result, they excelled at school, and they grew to be responsible young adults. Mia, our eldest daughter, became a role model for Lulu and Lorenzo when she became financially independent at a young age.

Carlos was a strong leader in civic organizations and at church. We were involved in fundraising concerts and cultural presentations that kept the young Filipino generation aware of our roots and proud of where we came from. Carlos was a gregarious extrovert, and we enjoyed bonding with friends on weekends over good dinners and music. We were like a big happy family in this small community that we built for ourselves.

Unexpectedly, several years later, as we went through life's twists and turns, the winds of change caused Carlos and I to grow apart. The song of life that we had sung beautifully together for many years gradually faded, and unwanted discords and dissonances came to a crescendo. We became strangers in a strange land. Despite the counseling sessions we went through, we knew our marriage was coming to an end. My daughter Lulu saw me crying one day, and she cried too as we hugged each other. She became my strength and assured me that she would be there for me all the way.

In the close-knit Filipino culture, we have strong family values. Most of us honor our vows "till death do us part." Yet in our thirtieth year together, Carlos and I both realized that it was best for us to go separate ways. We officially got our divorce on February 3, 2003— the same date my son Lorenzo had been born twenty years earlier. Unbelievable! That day was a tale of both triumph and tragedy for me. The experience became my big turning point. I spent the next few years finding the wisdom behind it all.

Life has taught me that we make choices for the good of everyone. Through time, people change, and what worked in the past may not necessarily ring true in the present. If we want to make better choices, we need to be open to what life is teaching us and have the courage to put those lessons into practice. Instead of blaming another, we should take full responsibility for our own actions and do what's best for us.

True happiness comes from following our inner voice, and any path that compromises our truth will put us out of sync with the true people that we are meant to be. No one else needs to understand our personal journeys. We do not need to conform and be like anyone else. One's individual path is not anyone else's path, and one's personal story may not ring true to another. Only our hearts know what's true for us.

Like chapters in a book, life has cycles of beginnings and endings. Carlos and I were meant to be together for thirty years to fulfill a divine purpose. That being completed, new doors were opened for us to focus on new visions and explore life without each other. Everything happens for a reason. I looked at the wisdom the past had taught me and approached my new chapter as a clean slate, keeping my mind positive as I reassured myself that everything was going to turn out for the best.

Chapter 5

DISCOVERING HOW TO
SING MY OWN SONG

I did not come to that hopeful view of my situation right away. Dark moments changed my life tremendously. Having lived a life of comfort and ease, I felt that I had now fallen from the tower that had housed me all those years. I was on my own. The experience forced me to increase my awareness of life's realities and understand the intricacies of this journey.

Change inevitably happened. I felt a strong sense of inner strength and empowerment being born in me. My soul was discovering how to sing its own unique song. With my newly acquired independence, I summoned the confidence to do what it would take to rebuild my life. I learned to trust myself. No matter what I was faced with, I would do what it took to get where I wanted to go.

I slowly walked away from my familiar community and went down a new path to the beat of my own drum, leaving behind what no longer resonated with me. My situation had taught me to live life with its imperfections, without complaining, blaming, and judging others, patiently doing what I could to further my growth. I understood the lessons presented. Things of the past were accepted and forgiven.

Also at this time, I remembered what the nuns had taught me growing up. Everything came back to me full circle. They had preached that life is about taming the ego, the false self, in order to allow the love of God to manifest in our lives. Too often, we resent things that are beyond our control. When we learn to transcend from the ego self and allow God to take control, things will flow in accordance with the divine plan.

Those were difficult things to start with. Yet I meditated and prayed each day and learned to trust that everything I needed to do would be revealed to me in the way it was intended to be. Gently listening with faith to the voice within, I felt empowered. Fears, worries, and doubts slowly melted away, and I came to understand what my soul was telling me. I knew that doubt meant giving away my power to my ego; I would attract what I was afraid of. So I put all my faith in God that things would be given to me that were best for me.

My faith has been my strength through all of my life. Many years ago, when I was newly married, Carlos fell mysteriously ill, and the doctors could not tell what was wrong with him. All the medical tests showed nothing wrong with him, yet he was having excruciating stomach pains. He did not eat for days and got weaker and weaker. At the hospital, the doctors wanted to do an exploratory surgery on him, but I refused. Instead, I brought Carlos back home.

About that same time, I was expecting my first baby, Mia. I was very much overwhelmed and stressed out. I didn't know what else to do but surrender everything completely to God. I prayed to the miraculous Holy Infant Jesus of Prague, or Santo Nino as we call Him. Within hours, Carlos began to sweat, and he told me his stomach pains were gone. Carlos was healed through faith!

Years later, a similar thing happened to my second daughter, Lulu, when she was four years old. She was in the hospital for days, was not eating as well, and was crying endlessly due to severe stomach pains. When the doctors could not find anything wrong with her, I brought in a statue of the Holy Infant Jesus and put Him at Lulu's bedside. I allowed God to heal her. She started to calm down, and the next day, we happily brought her home.

Days before our family left the Philippines for the United States, the Holy Infant Jesus appeared to me in a dream and told me that He wanted me to bring His statue with us. He was to be dressed in our native *barong*. To this day, the Holy Infant Jesus keeps me company at my home, which makes me feel safe and at peace. In His honor, Mia and Lulu's middle names are Nina.

Remembering these miracles gave me the inspiration and courage to approach the property manager of the building that Carlos used to rent for one of his law offices. I shared with this lady my sad story and told her that I wanted to rent a unit to open a music school. I had no money to start with; I asked her about the possibility of paying my rent later, when revenue started coming in.

The lady was quiet for a while, then expressed how deeply moved she was to hear my story. She revealed to me that she had never done this before, but she was willing to help me. Alleluia! This angel was God-sent. Unbelievably, she gave me two units to use for free until I was financially able to pay. I am forever grateful to this beautiful soul. Because of her help, I was able to grow my business successfully. On top of that, I was able to buy a new home for myself within a year.

Do you believe in miracles? I truly believe that when you let God, our Divine Source, empower you, you will be amazed to find a symphony of miracles happening to you. How fortunate is the person who possesses the awareness that miracles, which we often see as coincidences, are manifestations of God's presence in our ordinary, everyday lives. Whenever we pray, we are speaking to God. And when we receive the bounty of what we ask for, God is speaking to us. To be attuned to these moments is to be fully aware that God is always here for us.

When we are aware of and constantly guided by faith and the voice within, life flows with ease and grace. We calmly allow God to take over and let the ego step aside. We experience each day in tune with our divine purpose. We attract the best of what is possible, for life will harmoniously dance with us, showering us with synchronistic moments that will bring miracles into our lives.

What's also profound is the awareness that in each moment, we are the ones creating our own reality. We are not victims of circumstance. Those who see themselves as victims keep blaming others for their situation, which keeps them trapped and unable to realize their full potential. When life falls apart, it is a sign that God is inviting us to a far more beautiful life experience that is meant for us. Everything is meant to lead us to our highest good.

Chapter 6

THANK YOU FOR THE MUSIC

The song "Thank You for the Music" by ABBA sang in my heart for days while I was excitedly building my school, called Rising Stars Music and Performing Arts. My music programs were well accepted, and within months, I was able to expand by adding more teachers for piano, voice, strings, woodwinds, brass, and percussion, as well as dance classes. We formed a performing group called Glee, a song-and-dance group. God was very kind. In return, I gave back to the community by doing fundraising concerts to help those in need.

Following my passion is the best thing I have done for myself and others. It's not a job, it's a labor of love and a service to the community. Doing what I love to do, I am full of delight and joy. I am able to express the loving colors of my soul through the gift of music. With my own children now fully grown and living on their own, performing, teaching, and managing Rising Stars Music and Performing Arts have become the most fulfilling things for me to do. Since I have committed myself to this calling, I have been able to demonstrate the language of my heart to its fullest potential. Love, the essence of my being, has revealed itself through my sincere interactions with parents and students. In return, I receive appreciation and loyalty from them. They refer my school to their friends and give me five-star Yelp reviews.

My heart is filled with gratitude to my mother for passing on to me the gift of music. I now am blessed to share this gift not only with my children and grandchildren, but also with the community I serve. At an elementary school where I taught music appreciation classes for many years, I have had fun directing musical plays at Christmastime. I have played the piano for different choirs at church services. My soul has also found fulfillment in supporting others through fundraising concerts for schools, churches, and charitable institutions, as well as for victims of calamities in the Philippines.

A family who sings together stays together through all the good times and challenging times in their lives. Music, as always, has kept our family close. My children are very supportive of me at events. They have become the faces of Rising Stars Music and Performing Arts as they lead our student stars in shining at recitals, concerts, and performances at festivals, shows, and sporting events. Successful in their own business careers, my children are passionate about sharing their hearts with the world through the gift of music. Each of them has their own unique talents to share.

Mia, with her husband, Larry, is dedicating her life to helping autistic kids, and is a songwriter who also loves to sing. Classically trained, she won piano competitions during her student days and was a keyboardist in different bands. Both Mia and Lulu have master's degrees in business.

At only eight years old, Lulu won a national singing competition in the Philippines and appeared on a children's television show. She is the heart of Rising Stars Music and Performing Arts, playing an active role as a vocal coach, choreographer, event planner, and emcee for events.

Lorenzo, who studied at the American Musical and Dramatic Academy in New York, is a singer and an actor who loves to perform in musicals. He was the vocal headliner on Carnival cruise ships for years, performing for thousands of people all over the world. Multitalented, he is also in business and loves to write.

My five grandchildren—Alana, Heaven, Marquise, Teri, and Manny—also have our musical genes. They love to sing and dance, aside from excelling in sports and academics. On a Nickelodeon show, these smart kids won a competition together and brought home an amazing amount of money, which they happily shared among themselves. Teri, Lulu's daughter, is our promising star. She has sung the national anthem at sporting events, like a Lakers game.

Every child who becomes part of our Rising Stars family is taught not only musical skills but also confidence in themselves through performing at our events. We also instill in them the ability to express themselves through music coming from their hearts. Children who have regular musical training show improvement in their concentration skills, making them smarter at school. This has been scientifically proven through research and studies done by music therapists.

Music is a universal language that speaks to everyone when words cannot. It is through the power of music that we come to understand each other, no matter what culture we come from. As a young child, I enjoyed playing different kinds of music from all over the world. It was fascinating to me, like reading a story in a book. Playing the works of Bach, Mozart, Beethoven and others gave me a vision of what Europe was like. I dreamed that one day I would travel the world. Each summer for seven years now, I have accomplished this dream with my soul partner Marty. Europe still fascinates me with its rich culture as expressed through art, architecture, and music.

From the time we are born, music is introduced to us through the lullabies our mothers sing. Music is there all our lives, from nursery songs to love songs to the requiems that accompany our souls' journeys home to our Creator.

The magical power of music is endless. We express our feelings through music by playing instruments, singing, and dancing. Music has the capacity to make us feel younger, for it has a healing effect on our emotional and physical pains. It has the power to awaken our creativity and imagination, making us soar to our own magnificence. Music is a form of entertainment that uplifts our spirits, relaxes and soothes our souls, brings harmony to our relationships, brings rhythm into our daily lives, and enables peace in the world. Most of all, music brings us together as one big family every time we honor God through songs of worship.

I am very grateful each day for being an instrument of God's love through the gift of music. Thank you for the music!

Chapter 7

MELODY FOR TWO

How do perfect souls show up in our lives? Before I met Marty, I made a commitment to myself to continue my life journey with someone who was on his spiritual path. So I decided to work on my own reawakening to my spiritual truth. Amazingly, what came out of the experience was deeply profound. I realized that the quest for the right match is a quest for one's own wholeness. It is our relationship with God and our divine selves that holds the key to finding a soul partner. A person who is with a soul partner has embraced the divine within and the gift of unconditional love. Soul partners find themselves in an uplifting relationship, for they only seek the best of each other for their spiritual growth.

The most important relationship of all is a person's relationship with himself or herself. To find the right partner, you need to truly know who you are and what you are looking for. If you are wearing a mask to impress others and feel accepted, you are not being true to yourself or to your potential partner. When you truly love yourself, you are good to yourself and you create what is best for you. You don't allow others to define you and cross your boundaries through their limiting opinions of you. You treasure the love you have for yourself—for if you don't have love for yourself, how can you share love with someone else? You are emotionally secure. You don't need someone else's approval or bank account. And mostly, you enter into a relationship because you find a reflection of your true self in this being.

When I first met Marty, I saw a warm, friendly person who was full of enthusiasm and zest for life. I intuitively saw a loving soul who was passionately a creative expression of God's love. I was fascinated when he told me he was having Wisdom Healing Circle meetings at his home to help spread the message of love to this planet. He was surely on his spiritual path, and I felt we were kindred souls right then. Marty appreciated that I was childlike, and that warmly captured my heart.

Some people say opposites attract. This applies to Marty and me. A gregarious extrovert, Marty finds himself at home with my calm, peaceful attitude. We come from different worlds with different backgrounds and lifestyles. We have brought a perfect balance to the relationship as we bring out the best of ourselves to each other.

What's most endearing about Marty is that he is the most loving, thoughtful, kind, caring, and appreciative person I have ever known. Not a single day passes by without him expressing his deep appreciation for who I am and what we have brought to each other's lives. He's full of surprises; there's never a dull moment with him. Above all, he and I have a strong soul connection. Soul to soul, we mirror each other in many ways.

We are in tune in our love for spirituality, and we enhance this by attending workshops and conferences across the country. On weekends, we read to each other words of wisdom from our favorite spiritual teachers and share how they relate to our lives. We also love to travel, so once a year we go to different places in the world, where we always have a lot of fun and adventure.

Marty and I enjoy music from different genres. He brings out the rock person in me while I introduce classical music to him. We love going to concerts, as well as attending Broadway musicals most weekends.

Sadly though, as in any relationship, Marty and I went through rough times that caused our relationship to break up. In the third year of our relationship, Marty's outbursts about past unresolved issues would hit him whenever he was confused and stressed out, which was a totally new experience for me. Our relationship suffered. I felt boundaries were crossed when I found out he was complaining about our private issues to others.

I tried to understand what was going on and asked for clarification. Marty misconstrued my intentions and got very upset. His behavior reminded me of what he had told me years earlier: he'd always had problems with relationships, having gone through a lot of broken relationships as well as two divorces.

I spent three months dealing with the difficult situation. Marty refused to go counseling with me. I took the conscious choice to break up with him, to give him space to reflect on his emotional baggage. He was shocked by what he thought was a sudden decision, believing everything was fine between us.

I spent this time in my life finding the wisdom behind the situation, accepting the unexpected bumps without any judgment or resentment. It made me understand that no matter where we are in our spiritual journey, discord and arguments are still bound to happen. Keeping a harmonious relationship entails constant taming of the ego and honoring each other's differences through mutual respect and good communication.

We have no control over what comes from another person. We only have control of our reactions to situations. We cannot wait for the other person in order to experience a fulfilling relationship. We own our power; it begins and ends with us. We don't allow any person, place, or thing to have power over us. If we want a person to change, we must be the change that we want, since the other person will not change unless they want to. When we make our own change, everything around us will eventually change.

Surprisingly, Marty called me nine months after the breakup to greet me on Thanksgiving Day and ask if we could meet. We decided to celebrate his birthday belatedly with a dinner, so we met one evening at our favorite Japanese restaurant. For a present, I gave Marty little souvenirs, pictures, and postcards from my Hawaiian vacation that year with my son, Lorenzo. Marty expressed how each item meant a lot to him. We had a real, heartfelt sharing about what we had each learned from the breakup.

I eventually came to understand that Marty had unresolved abandonment issues and always needed attention to fill his emptiness. He had felt deprived of a mother's love growing up, when he was sent away to military school. He still felt a void within him in his relationships with women, regardless of the many sessions of counseling he went through. He always felt insecure and always needed validation from women. Though he liked their company, he hardly ever had long-term relationships.

Marty and I were already senior citizens when we met, and it was shocking to me that his childhood emotional scars had stayed with him all those years, eventually sabotaging our relationship. During our talk, I reassured Marty that I accepted everything about him because love is unconditional. When Marty heard those words, he found emotional healing within himself, and we happily got back together.

We had a wonderful time reviving what we had lost. Then, a few weeks later, I received angry, vindictive messages from one of the women Marty had seen during our breakup. She even wanted to physically confront me. She also berated Marty, saying, "Go back to your mother. She's old."

Life is simple. Any harmony or discord is a reflection of how we feel about ourselves. Marty made me understand that for a long time, he did not know how to love himself. He sought love from women in the wrong places, so most of his relationships with them turned out to be chaotic and full of drama.

This made me realize that no matter what life stage we are in, we never stop learning from each other. Whether it's with a partner, family member, friend, or business associate, relationships are the best teachers to help us become our best, truest selves.

We are all works in progress. Rather than resent those who are judgmental of us, it's always best that we don't take things personally. People have their own issues, and life is too short to allow their negative opinions to rob us of our joy.

By simply staying calm and not having anything to prove to anyone, you become the bigger person. It is not a sign of weakness; it is a sign of inner strength. You are not giving your power away. You are operating with the Divine Power, who created only goodness for you. When you allow this power to be in you, miracles happen. You will attract people and circumstances in harmony with you.

The greatest gift we can ever give to others is our own happiness, for when we are happy, anyone we are connected to benefits. Happiness does not depend on what others do for us. Nor does it depend on our attempts to please others. No matter how hard we try, we fail to please others, we fail to please ourselves. Happiness comes from our own emotional balance, from being in harmony with our inner selves.

When love is given and received fully by both partners in a relationship, it becomes the strongest connection anyone can have. You are soulfully aligned with one another, and the bond is lasting. Marty and I have learned a lot from our breakup and are very grateful for what we have in this last phase of our lives. We have learned to listen, honor each other's opinions, and resolve any miscommunication peacefully. Marty has also learned how to love himself unconditionally and not to be hard on himself. He has been attending classes called A Course in Miracles, which has taught him tremendously about loving and serving others. Never controlling each other, we have learned to accept each other's differences and give each other the freedom to be who we are. With our hearts open, we share our innermost emotions without judging and putting each other down.

It is awesome to see the new Marty emerge as a person full of love and compassion for people. Marty has turned his past painful experiences into blessings by teaching Wisdom Healing classes and writing books about his life story. This work heals him and helps empower others. He shows love and compassion for the homeless by donating to and supporting fundraising projects for them. His figurine collection—lighthouses, rhinoceroses, and Frosty the Snowman—helps fill the void from his lost childhood of not feeling loved. It gives him positive energy and empowerment. The lighthouse represents himself, his third eye radiating to be a light to others. The rhinoceros is his symbol of courage and strength in achieving his goals. Frosty the Snowman is the child in him, who smiles at the world to make everyone feel good.

Once, a girlfriend who was bothered by Marty's collections wanted to throw all the figurines in the dumpster. That ended the relationship quickly. I believe people go from one relationship to another in search of the right match, but as long as we wish things to be different and don't accept each other, relationships can't flourish.

Marty and I now see each other as best friends and soul partners. It's incredible how opposite personalities coming from two different worlds are now more in tune with each other.

We hope our simple story helps spark a life of harmony and peace in everyone.

Chapter 8

CELEBRATING LIFE

"Fantastic" is the best way to describe my life in 2018. It started with my family honoring me on my seventieth birthday in early March. The party was held at a reception hall on top of a hill in view of the mountains in Los Angeles County.

The ambience was elegant. The tables and chairs were very festive in gold and white, and the rose centerpieces adorned with intricate musical notes made everything truly classy. The themes of the night were uplifting: family, love, and music.

To the tune of Mozart's theme "Elvira Madigan," I made a grand entrance with my grandsons Marquise and Manny as my escorts, followed by the rest of my family. We had a champagne toast, and it was heartwarming to see relatives, old friends, new friends, and guests gather to celebrate my event. They were graciously treated with lavish food, wine, and music. I cherished the outpouring of love from my family as they sang heartfelt tributes in a family concert. Every family member also shared what I truly meant to them. In the finale, they got me up from the audience to sing "Thank You for the Music" with them. I followed this with an impromptu dance to the strains of "Dancing Queen," making me officially the queen for the night.

I was deeply touched by the generous words from sincere friends who gave their own testimonials, from the mayor's appreciation for my service to the city of Walnut to Marty's open expression of his love for me in front of 120 guests.

There was dancing and a lot of fun the whole evening. The guests expressed their sincere appreciation for what they described as a delightful treat from my talented children and grandchildren. Some made comments that it was the best party they had ever attended. It was indeed the best treat I have ever had, and a night to remember for the rest of my life.

One of the guests featured me on the front cover of *Manila Up*, a Filipino international magazine, and wrote articles about me and my talented children for their Mother's Day 2018 issue. That was icing on the cake!

Many months later, I was one of the honorees at a big event recognizing Filipino Americans who made a difference in the community. I received an award for inspiring kids in the field of entertainment, music and the performing arts. It was an elegant night, the gentlemen wearing black ties and the ladies formal evening gowns. I felt like an Academy Award winner.

Now in 2020, in the midst of the chaos happening this year, Marty and I finished writing our book *Journey of Love* and had it published. Our life lessons are our humble contribution to help shed light on people's lives. I also inspired my daughter Mia to co-write a song with me based on a melody that was singing in my dream one night. In my sleep, my subconscious mind was sending me messages to heal people's hearts through music. People were overwhelmed with racial problems in early summer and were protesting on the streets for social justice.

Mia and I collaborated in composing the song "One World in Unity," which became the theme of our Rising Stars virtual concert.

Lulu spearheaded the concert to raise funds for social justice and homelessness. Our talented Rising Stars students performed as well as some invited guests. At the finale, grand-daughters Heaven and Teri, along with their moms Mia and Lulu, sang together our song in beautifully, blended harmony.

It was gratifying to see my family carry out the vision in my dream. They are God's gifts to me, and they are my gifts to the world. What an awesome blessing to have my music heard through the music in their hearts.

Chapter 9

TIMELESS WISDOM

In Tune with Life

My birthday event gracefully ushered in a rebirth from the soul level. As I look back at the entire concerto of my life, I can see that every aspect was part of the divine plan to lead me to where I am right now. Every experience has led me to a higher level of awareness, joy, and contentment. From this vantage point, I live every present moment fully, as the best that can be.

I have learned to choose to have a positive response to challenging situations. Some of us repeat a pattern of blaming others for our failures. Life is like a school. Life gives tests, and unless we learn from our mistakes, we suffer. Every experience teaches us to make better choices and to have the right attitude. Whenever I choose to expect something good out of a situation, new doors are opened for me. Life flows with ease, in alignment with my desires.

The Power of the Present

The present is the point of power that creates miracles in our lives. Some of us are concerned about things of the past or about what will happen in the future, hardly paying attention to the present. By making peace with the present, we become one with life. I have found that this is the key to the art of living. It is the secret to youthfulness, success, and happiness. The more we appreciate each moment, the more God, our Divine Source, brings blessings at a perfect time and space.

Divine Purpose

I continue to express love in what I do, following my soul's calling to the unique best of own ability—through music. My divine purpose in being here gives me a sense of joy and inner peace, knowing that I am divinely fulfilling what I am here for. I am in love with life, beautifully turning everything into blessings to benefit everyone on this journey. I let things be without any judgment or resistance, always trusting that God gives us what's for the highest good of everyone.

Health and Well-Being

I see the wisdom and magnificence that graceful aging represents. When we embrace the years life has taught us, we glow with inner peace, joy, and contentment. Taking care of our well-being and physical appearance shows the love we have for ourselves as well as honor to our Creator. We cherish the bodies we live in, for they are living temples of God. I believe our bodies mirror our thoughts and emotions. By nourishing our bodies with loving thoughts and healthy choices that uplift our spirits, we inspire our bodies to smile back at us through the gift of vitality.

Gratitude

These days, I start my day off with a song in my heart, thanking God for the blessings of life and the joy of being alive. I no longer take things for granted. Each day we are given the chance to a fresh start in creating joyous, fulfilling lives. No one is too old to start something new and explore new things. No one is ever too old to be childlike, full of wonder, and perceptive through eyes of unconditional love. Each brand-new day, I ask God to make me an instrument of His love to everyone I meet. This puts a smile on my face as I feel the world smile back at me.

Taming the Ego

Life has also taught me that when we rise above our egos, our souls reach the higher dimensions of our beings. We come to accept reality and respond positively to things that are beyond our control. We no longer complain when things are not the way we want them to be. We no longer judge, blame, or have the need to be right and thereby triumph over others. We choose to be forgiving to those who hurt us, accepting peace as a sign of strength, not weakness. When the ego is tamed, we come to respect everyone for who they are, without any judgment, embracing one another as we rise above our differences.

The Infinite Journey

2020 is a critical time for all of us. We are facing a global crisis due to the coronavirus pandemic. Thousands of people have died and many more are infected by the virus. We are ordered to stay home to keep the virus from spreading, and businesses are closed.

Everything that happens to the world happens to us individually. We are all connected, and what happens to one affects the other. We need healing in our bodies, our hearts, and our spirits. We feel each other's pain as we become one big family helping one another. We are invited to reflect on what we value the most.

Staying home in compliance with the mandate, I get to appreciate the simplicity of life. I feel compelled to go into silence and listen to the voice of spirit. In timeless meditation, I blend with the divine like a beautiful symphony.

Spirit has revealed to me these profound, uplifting words of wisdom:

- We do not need to go into fear, for fear in itself is a virus. It is the ultimate dis-ease.
- There's a spiritual purpose behind the chaos that's happening right now. Through these difficult times, we have the chance to plant the seeds of our own greatness, bringing out the best of ourselves as we love one another and are of service to others.
- People who have an easier time are trusting the process, releasing control, and allowing themselves to surrender to the moment. Faith really counts. It's our spiritual muscle in this time of need.
- We are in a global metamorphosis. Like a caterpillar that emerges into a butterfly, our species is called to mature into a new awareness of ourselves, into an era of inner transformation.
- No matter how great we are, life can quickly be taken away from us. We are reminded that at the last moment of life,

nothing else matters. The soul does not care about earthly possessions—cars, houses, bank accounts, or fame. We will leave everything behind.

- Living life now, being our truest selves, means living from our souls—the God within us, where only goodness resides. It is only through this awareness that we can truly love and serve one another. It's what real wealth is all about. What is real never dies. The soul lives and loves forever.

The song "Fill the World with Love" echoed through the reception hall on the day my family honored me. I was in tears, deeply touched with joy upon hearing my children and grandchildren sing in unison from their deepest hearts. They summed up my life story through their song. They are my music. They are the ever-flowing melody of my life. And yes, my world of love has been best expressed by inspiring hearts and uplifting others to shine brightly through the gift of music.

This is not the conclusion of my story. This is just the beginning of a new dawn. New chapters are yet to unfold. *Journey of Love* is an infinite journey, an unfinished symphony.

The Time of My Life

From a vantage point I am standing tall
As I see the tapestry of life unfold before me.
It has been a fulfilling journey.
Yet I am not done.
For the music within me
Will keep on singing my whole life through.

Reaping the harvest from hard-won years
Of wisdom through life's agonies and ecstasies,
I am an avid learner in this school of life
As every experience nourishes my soul.

Like a river, I am serene where life leads me.
I surrender and I am at peace.
Living life at its best with ease,
And celebrating each precious moment
With grace and gratitude.
This is the time of my life!

—Aurora Belderol

My Precious Jewels

Alana

she's regal as she moves gently through life

she represents true beauty from within

through the years she's grown in confidence

and became a beauty pageant finalist

now she does modeling for fun

to me she's a queen

Heaven

her name is who she truly is

a touch of heaven in my heart

for she warms everyone with her presence

she is driven in athletics and academics

and sweetly endearing when she sings

Marquise

like his sister he is sports-driven

excels at school as well

talented and super smart

affectionate and loving to grandma

respectful and thoughtful too

to me he's a prince

Teri

singing is her forte

as she belts out the National Anthem

at a Lakers game and other sporting events

she's my Whitney Houston and Beyoncé combined

Teri the star got our musical genes at their best

Manny

Playful, funny and entertaining

full of charm and affection

and good looks too

he excels in soccer

Manny's our adorable lad

Jobey

my four-legged furry one

he is indeed man's best friend

as he embodies unconditional love

all of the way

I love you all!

—Grandma Aurora

One World in Unity

(Song)

We are lost, trying to find the cause
Asking for your guidance
And light through the darkness
Many have lost their lives
And became the sacrifice
Heal the broken-hearted
In a world of hatred

We are all God's children
Let's embrace our differences
We are all one family
One world in unity

As we begin to heal from within
It starts by understanding
We need to make some changes
And be more accepting
Everyone has pain and sorrow
But let's make a better tomorrow

And forgive those who don't know
The wrong that they've done
Release all the anger so we can move on

We are all God's children
Let's embrace our differences
We are all one family
One world in unity

—Aurora Belderol
and Mia Humphreys

PART II

MARTY'S STORY

Chapter 10

SCENES FROM CHILDHOOD

Growing up in the 1950s and 1960s was for me a very difficult and challenging experience with a lot of adversity.

My very first memory is from when I was six years old. I was in first grade at Montemalaga School. I got very sick, and the school principal wrapped me up in a warm blanket because I was shivering. He was kind and caring, holding me until my mother came to pick me up. I really appreciate this memory of a compassionate and loving school official.

After that experience, what I remember is being sent away to military school. That was extremely difficult for me; I was scared of the place. The house mothers and drill sergeants said to me, "Do you know why you're here?"

I said, "I don't know why."

They said, "You are here because your father and mother don't want you." Then they said, "You can't see your father and mother for six months. We are going to break the ties between you and your family."

Being a kid, I felt very sad, rejected, and abandoned. I cried in my bed every night for six months. I was traumatized and felt unloved by my family. I was at this school for most of my elementary years, and those were unhappy years for me. The only time that I liked was when I was playing sports, which I was good at. I also looked forward to seeing my mother on Sundays. She would take me out to the carnival, where I enjoyed playing the games and won a lot of stuffed animals.

I knew my mother loved me in her own way, but I was very confused as a kid. I did not understand why I was sent to live at the military school while my three brothers lived at home with my parents. I was only home four or five times a year, and I did not feel any bond with my family. In my heart, I resented that I was away from them.

I was told that I was a hyperactive child and I had been giving my mother a difficult time. At times when I was home with my family, I would run away because I thought no one understood me. All I needed was their attention. I always felt I was not good enough, and I did not feel good about myself.

When I was about ten years old, my father brought me to a psychologist for counseling. This person told me that the reason I was at his office was because I was a problem to my family. Out of anger, I stood up, broke the chair I had been sitting upon, and ran out of the office as fast as I could.

My mother had a lot of success as a beauty queen when she was in her prime. She was Miss Long Beach, California, in 1936, and Miss California runner-up in 1937. She was an intense, emotional extrovert. I know now that I was like my mom in many ways; that's why she had a hard time with me. She could not handle my temper tantrums as a kid.

When I was a teenager, I sold household products. My mother taught me to have a positive attitude and to believe in the power of positive thinking. She learned this from the famous writer and motivational speaker Norman Vincent Peale. I will never forget how she inspired me when she said, "Marty, you are a great salesman! You could sell snow to a snowman."

My father also cared about me. He was a quiet, gentle soul. At another time when I was depressed in my young life, he brought me to another counselor. This time, the counselor understood me. He allowed me to cry and express my feelings openly. That helped ease my emotional pain at that time. Whenever I needed help, my dad was always there for me.

Looking back, I think my parents did the best they could, and I am very grateful for what I learned from them.

Chapter 11

FINDING MYSELF
THROUGH FREEDOM

When I was fifteen years old, I came home to live with my family after being in boarding school for nine years. I had a difficult time adjusting to family life again. I asked my dad if I could get my own apartment. He said, "Yes, son, no problem."

He got me my first place to live on my own. Thank God. I felt free for the first time in my life. Freedom was the most important thing in my life because I had never had it before. The lesson here is never to take freedom for granted.

My life drastically improved once I was on my own. I was able to really connect with girls. I enjoyed sexual freedom in the late 1960s and 1970s. I was able to get out of my shell and became more outgoing as I found my own identity.

About this time, a classmate introduced me to the Fuller Brush Company. I became a salesman, earning between eight and nine dollars an hour. It made me proud, earning that kind of money as a tenth grader. This built up my confidence and self-esteem. With the money I earned, I was able to buy my first car for five hundred dollars in cash. That opened more doors for me, and I got more freedom and fun.

I was named salesman of the month many times, and I earned forty dollars a day several times. I received a gold Fuller Brush pin as a reward, and I still have it today, forty-nine years later, sitting on the wall unit in my family room. Remember that back in those days, the average price of a cleaning product was only $3.50.

I had a lot of good times. I lettered in varsity tennis as a tenth grader. Very few sophomores became varsity starters in athletics. As a team, we went to California Interscholastic Federation for the championship each year. I was very proud to be on the starting team from Rolling Hills High School.

I played tennis with the Austin family, the greatest family in tennis history with a thousand championships to their credit. I would go to their house for dinner and see all their awards and trophies in their showcases. I thought I was at a museum. They sold me some Jack Kramer crown rackets, which were the best at that time.

One more note about the Austin family: the youngest daughter, Tracy, won the 1979 and 1981 United States Tennis Opens, beating Martina Navratilova and Chris Evert. Tracy Austin was ranked the number one woman tennis player in the world, and became the first woman to make a million dollars on the tour in one year.

I graduated high school early in January, before the rest of my class. I got to graduate early because I had earned enough credits due to all my work experience with the Fuller Brush Company. I got to hang out with my friends, pick up girls, and go to the pier for fun.

I grew my hair very long and became a hippie. My hair was down to my ass after I didn't get a haircut for five years. The girls loved my long hair, which served me well. I had a lot of wild parties with thirty to forty teenagers at my apartment every weekend.

The only uninvited guests were the police, who broke up my party every Saturday night at 1:00 a.m. because the music was too loud. All I can say is I had the time of my life for three years with many different girls.

In August 1975, I learned to practice meditation from Maharishi Yogi, the same guru who taught the Beatles to meditate. My dad introduced him to me. I learned to do my own mantra and practice relaxation techniques.

At this time, I also met a beautiful girl named Amy. I was deeply in love with her for four years—the longest relationship I had had with a woman up to that time. Amy became my soul mate. She had blonde hair and blue eyes. I learned to ski when I went on camping trips with her and her family in Lake Tahoe and Yosemite. We had a really great relationship, and I loved her with all my heart. She was the first lady I lived with. We lived together for one year.

Amy wanted us to get married, but I wasn't ready. After four years, she said, "Either marry me now or I will leave you tomorrow." When she left me, I was brokenhearted for years. All I can say now is I wish her a nice, happy life. I am grateful for all the joy and love she brought me for those four years of my youth.

Chapter 12

WHAT MY CAREER TAUGHT ME

I was at the right place at the right time—I was the very first salesman in the United States to be hired to sell solar energy. I am so proud and honored to have pioneered the field in 1977. In 2018, California mandated that all new home construction must have solar energy panels by 2020. This is an awesome achievement, for it will bring a 50 percent increase in growth per year for solar energy revenues in California. This was the greatest job I ever had outside of teaching.

What my career taught me was never to give up when I was selling a product or a service. I learned persistence, tenacity, aggression, and ingenuity—doing whatever it took to get the sale. I had a tremendous amount of perseverance. There were two experiences that I will never forget.

The first experience occurred while I was selling solar energy for Reynolds Aluminum for eight years. I had an appointment with a husband and wife in Palos Verdes, California. This is the area where I grew up. I set a world record for a salesman by spending twelve hours at the couple's house.

Let me explain. They kindly told me that I reminded them of their son, who had been killed in the Vietnam War several years earlier. These beautiful people made me lunch. Six hours later, they made me dinner, and then dessert. They even asked if I wanted to sleep over in their son's room. That was too much. I explained that I was a married man, and I needed to go home to be with my wife. I sold them a solar system for their entire house that cost thirty thousand dollars, and this was in 1981. I earned three-thousand-dollar commission for twelve hours of work. That was the best day of my career, when I made two hundred and fifty dollars an hour.

The second experience was completely opposite in tone. I was working hard to get the sale again, pitching a solar system to a woman in Los Alamitos, California. Now, I have had extensive sales training—over two hundred classes, lectures, seminars, and conferences on how to sell and close a deal. I learned that the average person says no five to seven times before they say yes. I was always told by my sales trainers that if the customer keeps saying no, that means you've done a really bad job selling, and you better start over from the beginning.

So I was at the lady's house for six hours, trying for the tenth time to sell her a solar system. She asked me to leave her house. At that point, I asked her, "Where did I go wrong with you regarding this great investment? It will give you a 50 percent return on your investment. You will get all your money back in two years, and you will instantly add five thousand dollars to the value of your home. "I also explained, as I did with all my customers, "If you wait until later to install the solar system, you'll pay the whole cost and get nothing from the government. If you do buy now, you could receive a 55 percent tax credit from the federal government, as well as rebates from the gas company and the electric company. An investment of five thousand dollars will end up costing you two hundred, and you'll save that amount on your energy bills within two years."

The lady said, "If you don't leave my house right now, I am going to call the police."

I tried to sell her all over again. She got up and dialed the police department. I said, "Oh no, please don't do that. I am going to leave your house right now."

However, it had started to rain very heavily. I said to the very angry woman, "If I go outside, I will get wet and probably get sick. You wouldn't want that, would you?"

She went to her cupboard, got out a Hefty garbage bag, cut out holes for head and arms, and put the bag over my head. Then she said again, "Get out of my house or I'm going to call the police and have you arrested." So of course I left the house.

I just wanted to share with you what some of my sales experiences were like. You can see how different each experience can be.

In my thirty-five-year sales career, I had over ten thousand appointments with all kinds of people. I am very grateful I got to be a salesman, because I met so many people and learned a lot from them.

My father and my career taught me to work hard. My dad always told me, "Son, there is no substitute for hard work." He also said, "If you don't know how to manage your money, you won't have any." I was very successful in my sales career, working for eleven companies.

Everything changed, however, while I was working for Life Alert, the medical alarm system whose trademark line is "I've fallen and I can't get up." I was their salesman of the year. Things were really great. Then one day I was playing tennis in a tournament, and I noticed a large mass jutting out of my neck. I lost that final tournament of my tennis life.

The diagnosis was that I had stage four cancer of the neck. The doctor told me I had a 90 percent chance of dying within a year. I couldn't believe that in just a second, my life had changed forever. It made me realize that we shouldn't take life for granted. We should be grateful every day.

My family and I were devastated. I stepped down from the examination table, got on my knees, and went into a fetal position. I couldn't believe what had just happened. Remember, there is no stage five in cancer. Stage five is six feet under, you're dead.

After my second major cancer surgery, while I was coming out of the recovery room, I had an epiphany—an awakening, if you will. I told my brother Steve that I was going to change from being an egotistical jerk to a loving, kind, compassionate, caring person. I found myself in total transformation that moment in August 1999. Before cancer, I was narcissistic, self-centered, and selfish. I thought everything was about me. However when I got cancer, I didn't say, "Why me?" I said, "Why not me?"

After I went into remission, my doctors at UCLA told me that 50 percent of their patients saw the cancer come back within five years. They also told me most of their patients didn't learn anything from the experience and went back to their jobs once treatment and recovery were done. The doctors said, "Marty, you are in a very stressful profession as a salesman. We hope you find a less stressful career going forward."

I listened very carefully to what my doctors told me. After three major surgeries, three months of radiation, and two months of chemotherapy, I decided to retire at the age of forty-six. It was the best decision I made to extend my life. I am very thankful for how it turned out. Thanks to my three doctors at UCLA for saving my life, as well as to my family for all the love and support they gave me.

I am also forever thankful to the good friend who inspired me with his powerful words, "Adversity makes greatness." These words gave me the courage and the strength to beat cancer. About two weeks ago, this same friend called to inform me that he was very ill with the coronavirus. Feeling concerned, I reminded him about his powerful words that had made me strong when I had cancer. Today, I am happy to know that he is out of the hospital and recovering at his home.

Chapter 13

WHAT I LEARNED FROM MY SPIRITUAL JOURNEY

My spiritual journey started in October 2003, when I met a spiritual angel from God named Frankie. She was a beautiful soul who had more wisdom than any person I had ever known. Frankie was knowledgeable about metaphysics, a branch of philosophy that combines spirituality and science into one, leading to a healing and transformation from a dying self to a brand-new life. Frankie was into meditation and practiced it every day. She became my lover, teacher, best friend, and soul mate.

Frankie taught me tantra, the most powerful experience I ever had in my life. Tantra was invented in India three thousand years ago. It is about transcending both the sexual and spiritual planes as a means to enlightenment. Tantra brings more consciousness and sensuality into your life. It's a sacred, sensual awakening and healing experience.

Tantra teaches alignment through the seven chakras, the energy centers in the body. By chanting as we focus on the energy centers in our bodies, we improve our mind-body connections, keeping us balanced and calm.

Tantra is also about transforming day-to-day experiences into blissful celebrations. It teaches that everything you do can be a means to bring you closer to your own divinity. It is the belief that everything is divine—that when we are full of awareness, we are capable of revealing joy, no matter how negative our day is.

Frankie took me to many tantra classes. From those classes, I learned different ways to honor and respect my partner with truth and pure love. These experiences brought healing in many areas of my life. It was the most powerful thing I have ever felt in my body, mind, and spirit.

I learned a lot from Frankie in the two years we had together. Unfortunately, Frankie broke up with me and went out of my life. It broke my heart badly; it took me two years to get over her. I know people come into our lives for a reason. When it's time for them to go, they leave behind unforgettable memories and lessons for a lifetime. I am very grateful I had the experience of a great relationship with Frankie.

Chapter 14

THE WISDOM HEALING CIRCLE

Before Frankie left me, she told me to start a Wisdom Healing Circle. When I told her no way, she never gave up trying to persuade me.

Wisdom Healing is a practice of how to heal our hearts, minds, bodies, souls, and spirits. We can heal ourselves by our thoughts, feelings, and emotions. We learn how to practice awareness, consciousness, and self-healing techniques for good health and wellness.

I was the leader of the Wisdom Healing Circle meetings for almost eleven years, serving over three hundred people who came and went during those years. I wanted the circle to serve those who wanted to learn, grow, and heal in their lives. Most attendees treated it like a social event, which was not the purpose. I learned that I couldn't fix anyone. I just put the circle out there to spread wisdom, love, gratitude, kindness, compassion, joy, and peace. I served people and expected nothing. That has always been the motto of my spiritual journey, then and now. All I want to do is help, inspire, empower, and motivate others, without expectations.

The Wisdom Healing Circle was a labor of love. I never asked for a love offering or a love donation ever. It was a free event. The only thing I asked people to bring was a dish to share with others for the monthly dinner. Then we would listen to a guest speaker—I invited 130 of them over the years. I wanted to share with the people who came to be open to the possibilities of life.

The Wisdom Healing Circle started with two people at my house. It grew to fifty-four attendees and averaged thirty per meeting. I never advertised it; the circle grew through word of mouth. I am thankful for the time I had with these people, bringing them together to inspire, motivate, and empower them with my wisdom gained through eighteen years of experience on my spiritual path.

Our most popular evening was when we had a topic on A Course in Miracles. The guest speaker was a beautiful soul, a gifted human being who was not from this world. We kid one another that we are both aliens—she from a world in another solar system called Planet 9, and I from Mars. I always appreciated all the love she put out to the world every day. She taught us about being infinite souls in a temporary human experience.

Another beautiful experience happened when a couple in the circle suggested that we have a poetry night. At first, I was not excited about it. I had not written poetry before and was not interested in doing so. However, they convinced me to try it. It turned out to be very successful. Many of us wrote our own poetry for the very first time. Beautiful souls shared their creativity and expressed what was really inside them. That's what I love about poetry now. I discovered my creative side as I shared my heart and life experiences with others.

I am grateful for the Wisdom Healing Circle. Through it, I learned, grew, and healed. I matured as a person and became a better teacher and leader. Teaching is my greatest joy. I love teaching; it is a gift that keeps giving. I see people open up and share their feelings, thoughts and emotions. It doesn't get any better for me. I love it when people share their stories. When shy people become comfortable and feel it is safe to open up, it is a beautiful thing. I found that more profound than anything else.

One of my regular members didn't like a guest speaker who spoke about channeling from spirit. He got very angry and said, "Never bring a guest speaker like that again. You wasted our night." I knew a week later that this incident had happened for a reason. He confronted me again, and I thanked him for being my teacher. He told me he didn't want to be my teacher. Then and only then, I knew I needed to end the Wisdom Healing Circle. It was time for me to do other things, like be a teacher in another group, write books, and become a published author.

I am thankful to the beautiful soul who helped me see what my journey was going to be from that moment on. That was a very profound time for me, a defining, total transformation in my life.

Chapter 15

HOW I CREATED MY LIFE
AFTER THE CIRCLE

The poetry nights that we did for three years in the circle inspired me to write my second book, *My Love Story Book of Poetry*. I had written 110 poems in three months. An extraordinary amount of energy and creativity came over me like a powerful waterfall channeled through me from the spirit world. I kid you not. I had never felt that before. When I read my poetry book many months later, I couldn't believe that I wrote those poems. It was like some other energy source wrote them.

This experience inspires me to tell you another story. Before I wrote my first book, *My Amazing Transformation of Love, Courage and Wisdom*, I was very frustrated with the person I had hired to be my ghostwriter. I had to fire this person because the book was going nowhere. I was losing hope.

I then called my soul mate and best friend, whom I fondly call Rainbow Turtle (her real name is Gemma Aurora). I told her that I had let go of the ghostwriter. She suggested that I call a friend of ours from my Heart Math class at the Unity Church. Aurora told me with confidence that she felt this lady would be of help to me.

When I called our friend, she was excited and eager to start working. She got me motivated and inspired to write my first book. I am very thankful to her and to Aurora for inspiring me to take action. I am most grateful to Aurora for being with me on this journey in the last quarter of my life. She is a beautiful soul, my best soul mate, my best friend, and my life partner.

A few years before I ended the Wisdom Healing Circle, a friend and former president of the Osher Lifetime Learning Institute (OLLI) told me that they were having an open house at their center at California State University, Fullerton, California. OLLI is a continuing education program for seniors. I showed up in that memorable month of August 2013. I started to talk to the people around the table who were members of a mind, body, soul, and spirit group study called A Course in Miracles. The beautiful souls asked me what I was doing at that time in my life, and if I was a student at OLLI. I told them I was a community leader and had monthly Wisdom Healing Circle meetings at my home with invited guest speakers. One of the people asked what the Wisdom Healing Circle was all about. That question changed my life when I answered it. A distinguished gentleman overheard what I said, and he asked me if I would like to be a teacher at OLLI. I said yes instantly.

I have taught the Wisdom Healing class at OLLI for six years now. I love teaching. It's my greatest joy. I love it when my students get it. They range from eighteen to ninety-one years old. I have met many smart, nice, and educated people. As a student, my favorite classes are meditation and mindfulness and A Course in Miracles.

Meditation involved sitting in a comfortable chair for five to sixty minutes—whatever you can make time for—to relax and be peaceful and still while doing deep breathing. You close your eyes and just be. You can repeat a mantra, like do-re-mi or la-de-la, until you feel relaxed and calm. You put yourself "in the zone" and feel the joy of being good to yourself, finding total peace in those moments. Meditation has been proven to improve health and well-being as it reduces tension and stress. It lowers blood pressure and slows down the pulse rate. Practicing meditation on a regular basis will help you live a longer life.

Mindfulness means living in the moment—right here, right now. Being in the total present is a gift; that is why we call it the present. With mindfulness, we practice not dwelling in the past or worrying about the future. If you worry about the future, you will only be full of fear and anxiety. Remember, the future has not happened yet. When you catch yourself worrying, remind yourself to get back to this very moment, and live one moment at a time.

Being mindful is also about not judging other people. You accept them for who they are and are at peace with them, rather than arguing about who is right or wrong. The Dalai Lama says that if we are at peace with ourselves, then we will have more peace in the world. All things are possible if we believe they are.

After I ended the Wisdom Healing Circle meetings, I found more awareness about recreating myself for the rest of my life. I passionately disconnected myself from about thirty to forty members of the circle because I felt I had outgrown those souls as I moved on in my life. This totally empowered me to love myself and to alienate myself from people who were lost souls, negative in their ways. I started to hang out with like-minded, positive, beautiful souls.

The people in A Course in Miracles are some of the most positive people I know. Every time I am with this group, I feel happy, peaceful, and spiritually uplifted. Whenever I experience their weekly spiritual fill-up, I feel at home and calm in my life. I have taken this study for six years now, and my level of anger is the lowest level it has ever been. I can handle people and situations better than at any time in my life.

These beautiful souls share their personal stories about their journeys of peace and enlightenment. Everyone has a story. When we openly share our life experiences from our hearts and souls, we likewise share love, peace, joy, and wisdom with one another. That is why I enjoy and highly recommend this study group to everyone. It can change the way you look at things. I have learned that it's not what you're looking at, it's what you're looking through that matters.

A Course in Miracles teaches us to always come from love, not fear. Love is real; fear is illusion. I have also learned that FEAR stands for "false events and/or evidence appearing real." The study further teaches that ego is fear, anger, hatred, judgment, and jealousy. If you give energy to these negative emotions, things will only get worse for you. Love is the only answer to everything.

One of my mentors, the spiritual teacher Wayne Dyer, explained that EGO stands for "edging God out." It is important that we practice taming our ego selves every day. One way is by spending time walking quietly in nature. Nature helps keep us balanced and grounded, so we feel our connection with God. Another way is by having a good attitude, an attitude of gratitude. Let our attitude of gratitude be our never-ending prayer. I suggest that you make a gratitude list, writing down everything you are grateful for in your life.

My soul mate Aurora always reminds me of her motto, which is "Don't complain, blame, or explain." I believe that if we do less complaining, blaming, and explaining, we will have more peace. How we treat people is really all that matters. We need to treat one another with respect, love, compassion, and kindness. That's how we will find our bliss and enjoy healthier, longer lives.

Chapter 16

WHAT I LEARNED FROM TEACHING

What I have learned most from being a teacher at the Osher Lifetime Learning Institute is to become a better listener. I have always been a good talker, but before, my listening skills were very weak. Whenever I am teaching, I am a lot more mindful to listen to my students and not interrupt them. I let them finish their stories or comments without stopping their flow of communication. This enables me to learn a lot more about them and myself, as well as grow and heal.

Another important area I have learned about is how to practice sound healing. Sound healing is singing, chanting, humming, laughing, and listening to your favorite music. All of these promote vibrational energy that enters your body and gives you an internal massage. Research shows that if you practice sound healing, you can heal on a cellular basis. I practice this in my Wisdom Healing class. Wisdom Healing is about healing your mind, body, soul, and spirit by changing your thoughts, feelings, and emotions.

In my sound healing class, I teach students the art of vibrational energy healing. The first instrument I use is a drum the size of a very large plate. I beat the drum to the rhythm of a heartbeat (1-beat, 2-beat, 3-beat, 4-beat). This relaxes my students so they are calm, centered, grounded, and balanced.

The second instrument is a singing crystal bowl. It's like a wine glass: you rub your wet finger around it, and you get a humming sound. This creates positive energy vibrating through your seven chakras down your spine. It's amazing how the whole room vibrates whenever I play the crystal singing bowl.

The third instrument is a holistic steel drum that is designed like a turtle shell, perfectly tuned at 133 hertz. Whenever I play it, my students tell me that they feel like they're in heaven. They find themselves in total peace and tranquility.

In my years of teaching, I have learned to have more patience with people. I used to be an impatient man, full of anxiety. Whenever my students don't get what I'm teaching, I simply take my time and explain things to them in different ways. I have come to fully understand the statement that "patience is a virtue."

Teaching has taught me to care about my students. I have noticed that I have very loyal students who come to every class and don't miss a single time with me. I am very proud of them because they really want to be more aware and evolved spiritual beings with a lot of consciousness about what life is.

I ask my students what their purpose in life is, what the meaning of life is, and why we are here. Surprisingly, several students have said, "I will get back with you on that." It is a difficult question for some. When my father was in his early eighties, he would say to me, "Son, I have accomplished everything in my life, everything I wanted to do. I have no more purpose at this time of my life." Whenever he talked like that, he was very depressed. His depression got worse and worse until one day, he tried to take his own life. Thank God, I had my dad for a few more years. He died at eighty-eight years old.

The lesson I want us all to learn is to never stop having a purpose in life. Purpose will keep us going. We should live our lives with hope, faith, love, and gratitude. Never give up. This is my philosophy: never quit, no matter how hard life is. Keep creating things in your life and your life will be brighter and happier. When you're creating and recreating your life, you will continue to bring out the best of you, to benefit you and others. You will feel good about yourself, knowing you are living the best of who you truly are.

Now that I am on my third book, I have a tremendous feeling of confidence and self-worth, which I had struggled with during my early years. My self-esteem is at a higher level than ever before. I'm living a richer, more fulfilling life because I continue to create new things in my life as well as to recreate my life.

There are three important things to remember in life:

- Be inspired
- Be creative
- Take action—make it happen

You need inspiration to get you to do what you want to do, then follow your passion and have the courage to do it with no fear. Keep the momentum going. Strive to be in the vortex. Operate in your highest form of creativity with pure imagination, creating whatever you are most passionate about. Most people are afraid of taking the third step. They have fifteen excuses to do nothing; therefore, they accomplish nothing.

When I wrote 110 poems for my second book, *My Love Story Book of Poetry*, I was feeling like Niagara Falls. A tremendous waterfall of energy entered my body, mind, soul, and spirit. I was motivated to write my life in poetry, and I did it in three months—continuously, every day.

My advice is whenever you're motivated to create something, go for it and do it. This will change your life. You will feel a great sense of accomplishment, confidence, and fulfillment in your journey.

Chapter 17

WHAT I LEARNED FROM WRITING THREE BOOKS

What I have learned from writing my first book, *My Amazing Transformation of Love, Courage and Wisdom*, is that my life stories and lessons parallel the messages from the story in the movie *The Wizard Of Oz*. The Tin Woodman didn't have a heart, so he needed love. My book is about love. The Cowardly Lion was always scared. He needed courage. My book is about courage. The Scarecrow didn't have a brain. He needed wisdom. My book is about wisdom.

This all started when my soul mate Aurora (whom I fondly called Rainbow Turtle) and I went to a Hay House event in Maui, Hawaii, in April 2016, for a writers' workshop at the Westin Resort and Spa. It was led by Doreen Virtue, Reid Tracy, and Nancy Levin. We learned the ups and downs and pitfalls of writing a book. They all explained to us that the chances of a book being successful were very low. Hay House gave the five hundred or so attendees a set of guidelines about what they were looking for. They raised a high bar for a contest they were having. The contest was that if you submitted a manuscript following their guidelines, and your manuscript was the best, they would award you a publishing contract and ten thousand dollars.

Guess what? It scared me big time. I was afraid to even attempt writing a book. They really freaked me out about the possibility of becoming a published author. I looked at Aurora and told her that there was no way I was going to write a book. I was very discouraged and didn't think about it for six months.

Then in an OLLI class called Laugh, Learn, You're Retired, I spoke to my very best friend, Mark Geller, who has since passed away. He asked me how my book was going. I told him that I needed to hire a ghostwriter to help me write my story, because it was too difficult to write it myself.

A lady in the class overheard me and told me that she could help me—she could be my ghostwriter. A ghostwriter is someone you hire to write on your behalf, based on taping many hours of interviews with you. This lady said she had worked for the Associated Press and had written books herself. So I hired her, and she instructed me to tell my story into her tape recorder. She would not accept any gaps in the time frame of my story.

Well, I couldn't wrap my head around this concept. It freaked me out even more. This lady was so detached, I couldn't relate to her at all. After a few days, I texted her and told her that I'd had a change of heart.

Everything changed when, as I mentioned earlier, Aurora told me to call a friend. A miracle happened. This friend inspired me big-time when she told me she was willing to work with me. All it takes is one person to be a spark of energy and light to make a difference. I was very motivated and came to realize that I was going to write my book myself instead of having a ghostwriter. Our friend would be my assistant.

I wrote my book in twenty-three days—exhausting our friend, who edited and processed the book. So I hired another assistant, because I am not computer savvy. It took eleven months to get my first book published. It is a lot harder than you might think. I had to go through hundreds of hoops to get through the process.

However, through experience, patience, and determination, I have been able to write more books and have them published. *My Love Story Book of Poetry* and this book, *Journey of Love*, written with my soul mate Aurora, have all turned out easier. I also contributed to the book published by OLLI's poetry for pleasure class, *Poetic Gestalt*.

What I have learned most during this process is patience and more patience. The more patient I become, the better I am able to handle any situation. If anyone had told me three years ago that I would become a published author three times, I would have said, "I think you are crazy." I never dreamed I would become an accomplished, published author. I am very grateful.

Chapter 18

AURORA, MY INSPIRATION

I got to know Aurora through a friend from my Wisdom Healing Circle meetings. I first met Aurora on Sunday, July 29, 2012, and I just knew she was a very special woman. She was aligned with my spiritual beliefs and also very open to exploring new things. It is rare to find a total spiritual connection with the right person. Well, I feel that way about Aurora. She was different right from the start. Her full name—Gemma Aurora—truly speaks to the kind of person she is. She is a rare gem (Gemma) to find and she is the light at dawn (Aurora) to the people in her life.

Aurora's thirst for spirituality made me realize that she is who I have been searching for all this time. I soon saw that she is the most loving, peaceful, gentle, and tender woman I have ever met. She is calm and at ease with herself, and she always makes me feel I can be myself with her. This beautiful soul doesn't give me drama. She doesn't blame, complain, or explain. Most of my past girlfriends gave me a hard time and a lot of drama. They took advantage of me, using and abusing me. Some continually tried to change and control me, while others were very subtle in trying to manipulate me with hidden agendas. Aurora never does that.

I fondly remember the first few dates I had with Aurora. I took her to an arboretum for a beautiful walk in nature, surrounded by three thousand different trees and flowers from around the world. Then we sat under a Bodhi tree, which is known as the tree of knowledge and enlightenment. It was planted by His Holiness, the Fourteenth Dalai Lama, at the arboretum in 2000. Aurora was excited to learn about the Dalai Lama. I told her everything I knew about His Holiness, since I had attended his lectures five or six times, read many of his books, and listened to his CDs over the years. Aurora seemed very impressed by my knowledge, which I believe motivated her to learn more about me.

Another time, Aurora and I attended a dinner theater show. Up to that point, we had just been friends enjoying each other's company. Then an unexpected photographer came to our table. She told us to kiss while she took our picture. Aurora and I felt awkward as we looked at each other, but we decided to kiss anyway—for the very first time. It was heaven on earth in that moment! I felt we were guided by a higher power, and the photographer was the instrument to play Cupid for the miracle.

I knew from that moment on that Aurora was meant to be in my life. An amazing woman with so much love in her heart, she has been sent from above to teach me unconditional love. Soon after, I was inspired to give her a new special name: my Rainbow Turtle. "Rainbow" because she creates a lot of color and positive energy to my life, and "Turtle" because she is so calm and peaceful as she gently flows through life, savoring one day at a time. My Rainbow Turtle is a very nonjudging person, full of understanding and acceptance. She loves me for who I am. She is the best lady I have ever met in my entire life. That's why she is my best friend, life partner, and soul mate. She is my number one in the world. Did I leave anything out?

Being with Aurora is truly amazing. In her professional career as a musician, she has extended kindness and compassion to others, giving back to the community through fundraising concerts. Her concerts have raised thousands of dollars to benefit good causes, and she never took a cent for herself. To me, she is like a nun. She was raised in a Catholic school, and she is very nun-like in many ways. I'm not kidding. She's the purest soul I have ever known.

The spiritual journey that Aurora and I share is real and powerful. It is the glue that binds us together. We have the same spiritual mentors and love to read the teachings of Wayne Dyer, Esther Abraham-Hicks, Eckhart Tolle, Brendon Burchard, the Dalai Lama, Doreen Virtue, Edgar Mitchell, Jean Houston, John Kabat-Zinn, Louise Hay, Deepok Chopra, Mingtong Gu, and Neale Donald Walsh, to name a few. We go to conferences with the Institute of Noetic Sciences, known as IONS, for lectures on spirituality, science, and motivation. We spend our moments of relaxation listening to CDs that fill our hearts with love, wisdom, kindness, peace, joy, inspiration, hope, faith, and grace.

The music that we love and share is the icing on the cake. Our love for music is so deep, it's beyond words. Music brings us together. We love to go to concerts and Broadway plays. Aurora's favorite is classical music while mine is rock and roll. Well, what does that tell you? Opposites attract!

We are so opposite that even our astrology signs are opposite. Aurora is a Pisces while I am a Virgo. My moon has Pisces rising while Aurora's moon has Virgo rising. This was explained by a psychic: our opposing signs cause the energy in the universe to make the stars perfectly aligned in the galaxy. Isn't that incredible? We are opposite beings, yet we are aligned in our relationship. We even experience the same thoughts and feelings at the same time most of the time.

Aurora continues to amaze me every day of my life. She has the most positive attitude of any person I have ever met. She is always smiling and laughing at anything and everything. When life gets stressful, she simply retreats into her turtle shell for safety and security. She goes inward to recharge herself and bounces back at life always stronger, with a quiet confidence around her. That's the reason why she is always my strength and inspiration. Because she believes in me, I have been inspired to write my books.

I am so grateful to have a beautiful soul like Aurora in my life. She is sent from heaven in this last quarter of my life. I feel I'm the luckiest man in the whole world. I love my Rainbow Turtle with my whole heart and soul.

Chapter 19

LOVE, COMPASSION, AND UNITY

What I am learning from the coronavirus pandemic is that we need to step up as human beings to show more kindness and compassion to others.

I have seen a lot of people panic-buying and hoarding food as well as paper products. This shows me that some people care only about themselves during critical times. As we all know, we have major shortages of toilet paper and paper towels, and many food items are sold out. I know of several people who bought enough food and paper products for six months. That leaves many people, especially senior citizens like myself, short of supplies. As of the time of this writing, there are already millions of people worldwide infected with the coronavirus, and hundreds of thousands are dead.

I have never seen anything like this in my life. Most people are living in major fear and uncertainty. We are shut down as a world, and with the stay-at-home mandate, we are sheltering in place. If we have to go out to get food, we have to practice physical and social distancing from each other – six feet or more and wear masks.

This is a defining moment in our lives. 2020 is the time for us to see what's around us. We need to wake up to show our kindness and compassion to others. Let's help and support a friend, neighbor, relative, or homeless person. Give to others and expect nothing. John Wooden, the great basketball coach at the University of

California–Los Angeles (UCLA), once said, "You can't live a perfect day without doing something for someone who will never be able to repay you."

The other issue we are also having significantly this year is the issue of social justice. We need to relearn that we are all equal. No one is better than us, and we are no better than anyone else. We all need to do a better job in treating each other with dignity and respect, regardless of the our skin color or lifestyle choices. We need to stop judging people and discriminating others for who they are. Love and acceptance of each other are the major keys to heal our country and the world.

The pandemic and our social problems are our teachers to be better people and to have meaningful purpose in life. Let this be the miracle we have been looking for – the paradigm shift of consciousness, awareness, kindness, and compassion for all of us to give back to this beautiful planet that we all live on.

"E Pluribus Unum" is a Latin word meaning "out of many, one." It is in our United States Constitution and Bill of Rights. Our forefathers created this motto for us to be one people in unity. We all come from different cultures and we are all connected as one. May we all be one in spreading love, peace, and healing to each other and to the world!

My Soul Mate, Rainbow Turtle

I named my soul mate Rainbow Turtle.
Like honey, she is so fertile.
She is so sweet and kind,
I find her a rare find.

She is my best friend and soul mate,
The best girl on a date.
She is the best.
That's why I left the rest.

She is gentle on my mind.
I'm grateful she is mine.
Her colors are the best you can find.
And being a turtle, she takes her time.

She relaxes inside her shell.
Oh, she is such a belle.
I loved my Rainbow Turtle right from the start.
She has my heart, which is the best part.

She is so dear and has no fear.
She just loves me and all of mankind.
That's why she is the rarest of all time.

—Marty Cole,
from *My Love Story Book of Poetry*

The Lighthouse

Captain by the sea, it is 1983.
He loves fish because it is a lovely dish.

The keeper of the light
Never keeps it out of sight.
The seeds of the sea are all that you need.
It is an ocean of white healing light
That goes into the dark night.

He has the best attitude
Because he lives in gratitude.
The man by the sea
Is looking as fine as can be.
He comes from love in his heart
From the very start.

It's all about love—do not fear, my dear.
Back in '83, it was a very good year.
It was all about appreciating the sun,
Which, for me, made it all fun.

My life has been the best
Because I live it to the fullest
With zeal and with zest.

My purpose is to serve others
That's why I love the mothers.
My goal is to spread love and peace
So we can get violence to cease.
It's all about love, my dear,
So let's stop all the fear.

—Marty Cole,
from *My Love Story Book of Poetry*

We Never Die

We never die.
I believe we just fly.
I feel we will be in the earth, water, and air.
Our spirits will be everywhere.
I believe our memories will always be out there.
The future generation will know that we care.

We will be on the other side.
I feel it will be a blissful ride.
Don't worry, we'll just glide.
We'll never divide.
We will be with the divine.
It's only a matter of time.
Everything will be fine.

I love you all.
Let's keep loving in the afterlife
Like it's a piece of cake.
Keep loving forever for God's sake.

—Marty Cole,
from *My Love Story Book of Poetry*

Afterword

By Marty and Aurora

A s we receive the infinite freedom of choice to make life completely our own, the voices of our true selves have led us the way to be soul partners in this last phase in our lives. What makes soul partnership different from other relationships? Being in a soul partnership does not mean life is perfect. It requires working together on taming our egos and allowing unconditional love to lead the way. We are a work in progress every single day.

We, Marty and Aurora, have seen the light of who we are, with our strengths and weaknesses as well as our idiosyncrasies. Together, we have chosen to recognize life's blessings in the middle of life's unexpected twists and turns. We serve one another as instruments to growth and self-realization. Every single day, we express and allow our true colors to shine through. We continue to learn, for no matter how old we are, the voice of wisdom is ageless.

For eight years now, we have been there for each other at our happiest and lowest times, as soul partners living independent lives. It's the best path for us, to be a living expression of who we truly are.

In the midst of the coronavirus in this year of 2020, we are bonding closer than ever, though apart from each other. It is a great experience to meet at the park, take a walk together, and chat from six feet away. Following the mandate in order to stay healthy and safe, we wear masks and gloves. We have simple joys, listening to the sounds of the brooks, the swaying of the trees, the songs of the birds, and the croaks of the frogs. Nature seems to assure us that things will be better soon. At the end of our date, we pray for the world's healing and give each other a flying kiss. We feel spiritually nourished. In the midst of chaos, we are creating miracles in our lives.

Each day is a precious gift. We continue to love, laugh, and live one day at a time. Our mantra, "Let go and let God," guides us daily in what we do. When there's pouring rain, we choose to dance in it. For if we want to see the rainbow, we need the rain. And what a blessing to find that the pot of gold at the end of the rainbow is within us, the gift of each other.

CPSIA information can be obtained
at www.ICGtesting.com
Printed in the USA
BVHW030352161020
591139BV00005B/13/3